THE HOBBIT™

THE BATTLE OF THE FIVE ARMIES

The Movie Storybook

Houghton Mifflin Harcourt
Boston   New York
2014

King Thrór's once great kingdom of Erebor was legendary; its beauty lay under the earth, in its wealth of precious gems and seams of gold.

Thrór refused to listen to warnings from others that hoarding riches might bring danger. For the King Under the Mountain, the wealth he had amassed was worth more than his kingdom and the lives within it.

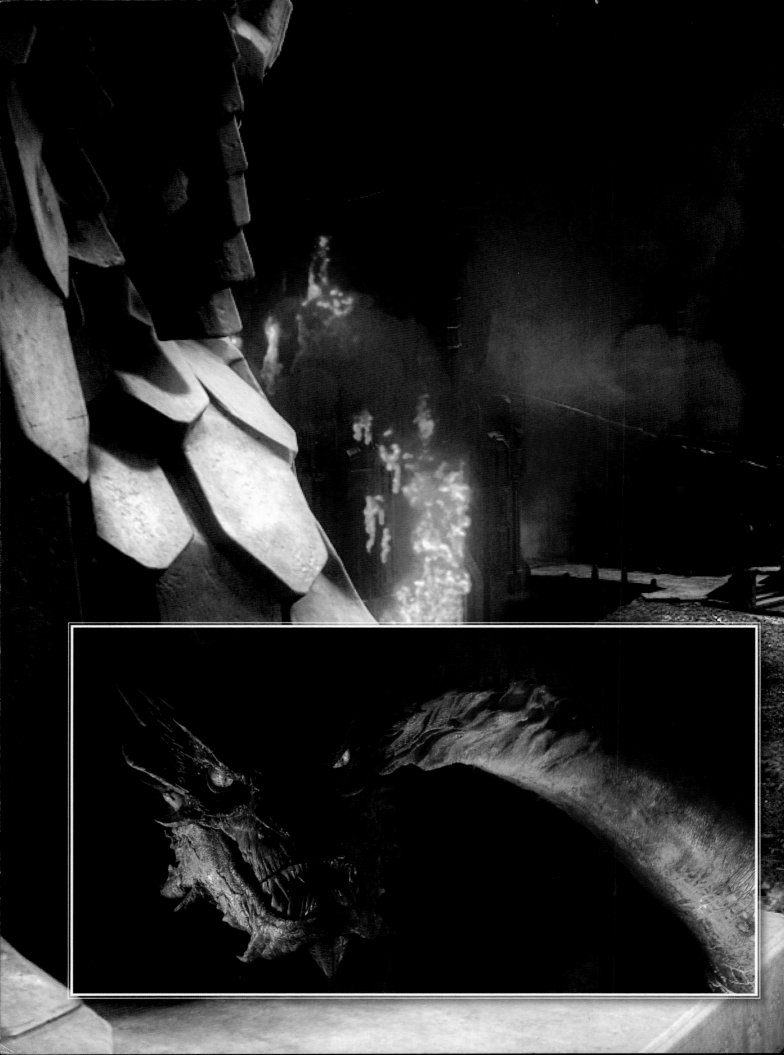

In the distant Grey Mountains, Smaug the Magnificent, a fire-drake from the North, was drawn to the great treasure hoard, for Dragons desire nothing more than gold.

After raining death and destruction upon the neighbouring city of Dale, Smaug turned his sights towards the mountain.

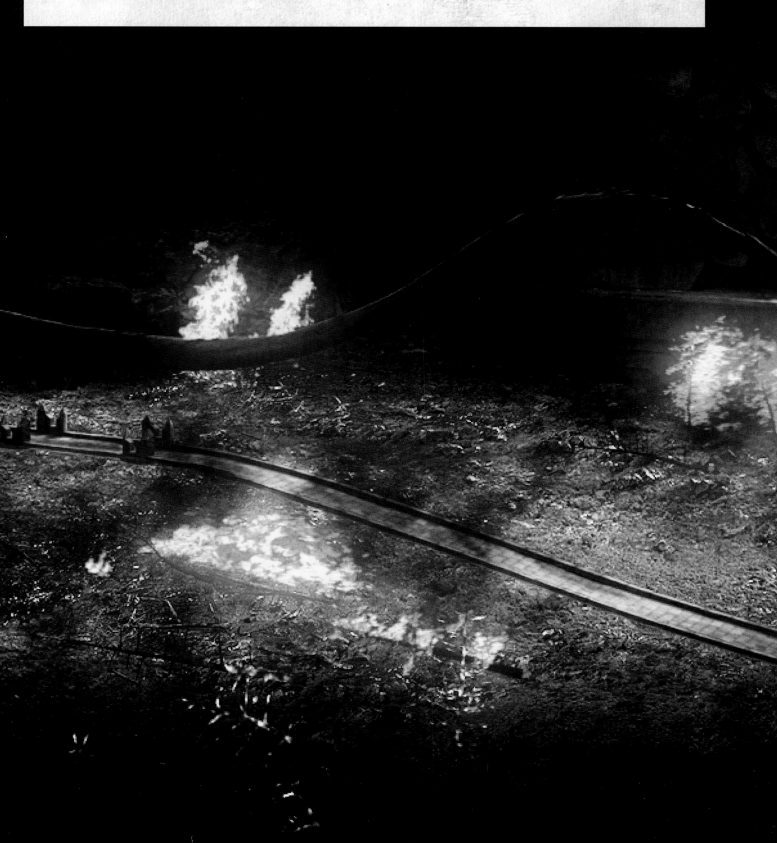

Driven from Erebor by the might of Smaug, Thorin Oakenshield, grandson of Thrór, led the remaining survivors in search of a new homeland.

The Dwarves tried to recapture the ancient stronghold of Moria. They fought a long and bloody battle with the Orcs that had overrun the once great Dwarven city.

Azog, a huge, pale Orc Commander, cut off the head of King Thrór, throwing it at Thorin's feet.

Enraged by the death of his grandfather, Thorin took off Azog's arm with his great sword. Believing that Azog died from his wounds, Thorin and his people assumed that the death of their king had been avenged.

Now, in order to be acclaimed as King Under the Mountain by the seven great Dwarf clans, Thorin needs to reclaim the Arkenstone – the 'King's Jewel'.

After years of wandering, his kinsmen scattered, Thorin gathers a small group of Dwarves and travels to The Shire.

At the request of Gandalf the Grey, Thorin's Company of Dwarves hire an unsuspecting 'burglar' named Bilbo Baggins, for the Arkenstone lies buried beneath the feet of the Dragon, Smaug.

With only a map and key to help them on their way, the Company set off from Bag End in the hope of once more reclaiming the 'King's Jewel' and the home that had been stolen from them.

The people of Lake-town have lived in fear under the shadow of The Lonely Mountain and its occupant. A dormant terror lies within, buried beneath vast swathes of gold…

But a new hope has been kindled, with the promise to return Lake-town to prosperity. Thrór's grandson Thorin, the rightful heir to the throne, has returned to reclaim his kingdom…

The King beneath the Mountain
The King of carven stone
The Lord of silver fountains
Shall come into his own…

And all shall fail in sadness
And the lake shall shine and burn.

13

After journeying across Middle-earth, Thorin's Company arrived at the secret door to Erebor just in time to see the end of Durin's Day – the only time of year the moonlight shines upon the hidden keyhole.

Using the key that Gandalf the Grey had given to him, Thorin unlocked the door by the light of the moon, and the burglar Bilbo was sent down to investigate…

In the quiet halls of Erebor, Smaug the Terrible was stirred from his slumber by the unassuming burglar Bilbo Baggins.

Using their knowledge of the mountain halls that were once their home, Thorin and his Company devise a cunning plan to rid the Lonely Mountain of Smaug once and for all.

Leading Smaug to the Great Hall, Thorin pours molten gold from the furnaces onto Smaug, believing that it will vanquish him once and for all.

Enraged, Smaug flies into the night sky, shaking off the gold from his wings. Knowing that the inhabitants of Lake-town had aided Bilbo and the Dwarves in their coming to the Mountain, Smaug flies towards Lake-town to unleash death and destruction.

The survival of the people of Lake-town hangs on a knife-edge.

Legend has it that Bard's ancestor Girion, the Lord of Dale, fired a black arrow from a windlance and dislodged one of Smaug's mighty scales. Now, only one black arrow survives, and its owner is locked away in the town's gaol…

After the destruction of their livelihoods, the former inhabitants of Lake-town must salvage what they can from the wreckage.

Aided by Tauriel and Kili, the survivors regroup on the shores of the lake. But when she is summoned by Legolas, Tauriel must leave them to attend to urgent business in the North.

With winter coming on, the survivors must seek shelter. Now the Dragon is dead, the people look to the Lonely Mountain and the new King Thorin to pay them the gold they were promised so that they might rebuild their lives in the ruined city of Dale.

Gold beyond measure, beyond sorrow and grief…

In the great halls of Erebor under the Lonely Mountain, Thorin Oakenshield broods over his gold.

He has reclaimed his homeland, but the Arkenstone, the 'King's Jewel', is still missing. Thorin commands his company to search night and day, until it is found.

Bilbo wishes, not for the last time, that the Wizard Gandalf the Grey was with them to offer his advice.

All shall come to dust and be forgotten...

Gandalf the Grey is being held prisoner in the ruined fortress of Dol Guldur by Sauron, known throughout Middle-earth as The Necromancer.

Sauron is keeping his prisoner alive to seek out the truth as to who holds the three Elven Rings of power.

Three rings for the Elven Kings under the sky, seven for the Dwarf Lords, in their halls of stone...

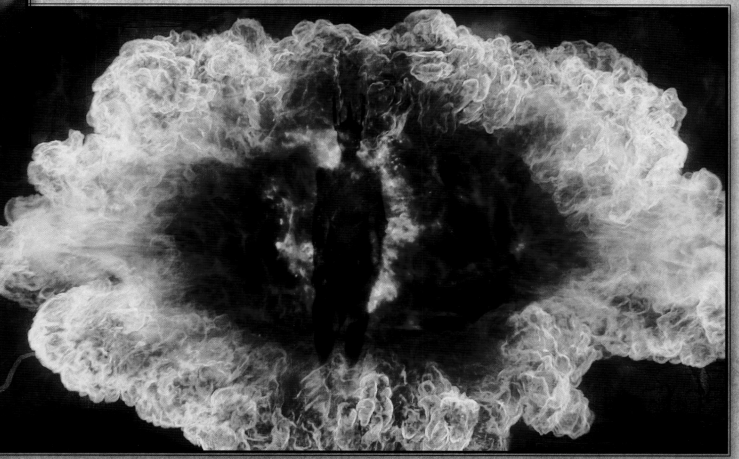

As Bard and his followers set up camp in the ruins of Dale, they prepare to face Thorin and his Company of Dwarves at the gates of Erebor.

Little do they know that the King Under the Mountain has been corrupted by 'Dragon sickness' – a curse that lies upon the treasure that Smaug had brooded over for so many years. And Thorin Oakenshield cannot stand to share even one gold coin, no matter who he has promised along the way…

King Thranduil of the Woodland Realm once struck a deal with Thorin's grandfather Thrór, to make his queen a necklace. The necklace was encrusted with rare white jewels, known as the Gems of Lasgalen. But as the rift between the Elves and the Dwarves deepened, Thrór refused to give Thranduil the necklace.

Now Thranduil too marches to the Gates of Erebor with an army of Elves, seeking the return of what he calls the heirloom of his people.

On silver thread was strung the light of stars.

Holed up inside the mountain, Thorin orders what is left of his Company to barricade the Gate to protect his beloved gold against the onset of the outside world.

Thorin confides in Bilbo and tells him that he believes that a member of the Company has betrayed him, and that they have stolen the Arkenstone. Bilbo is taken aback by the change in his friend; he fears Thorin is descending into madness.

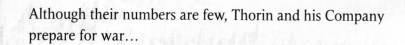

Although their numbers are few, Thorin and his Company prepare for war…

I will not part with a single coin – not one piece of it.

Meanwhile in the North, Bolg – the spawn of Azog the Defiler – prepares to unleash a devastating weapon to once and for all wipe out the line of Durin and secure The Lonely Mountain as a stronghold.

Escaping his imprisonment in Dol Guldur, Gandalf must warn Thorin Oakenshield of the army that marches upon him.

As the inhabitants of Lake-town and the Woodland Elves gather at the gates to negotiate with the Dwarves, Bilbo escapes to meet with them in the middle of the night. Worried for his comrades, Bilbo attempts to strike a deal with Bard and Thranduil to prevent the war that is about to ensue.

Compared to all the treasure in Erebor, Bilbo offers something that is much more valuable: the promise of peace instead of the death and destruction the people of Middle-earth are about to face.

I know Dwarves can be obstinate … and difficult, but they are also brave and kind and loyal to a fault … and I would save them if I can …

In a surprising and sudden onslaught the huge armies of Azog attack the Lonely Mountain.

Their numbers are so great, the only hope for the free peoples of Middle-earth is to unite as one, and for the rift between the Dwarves and the Elves to be put aside.

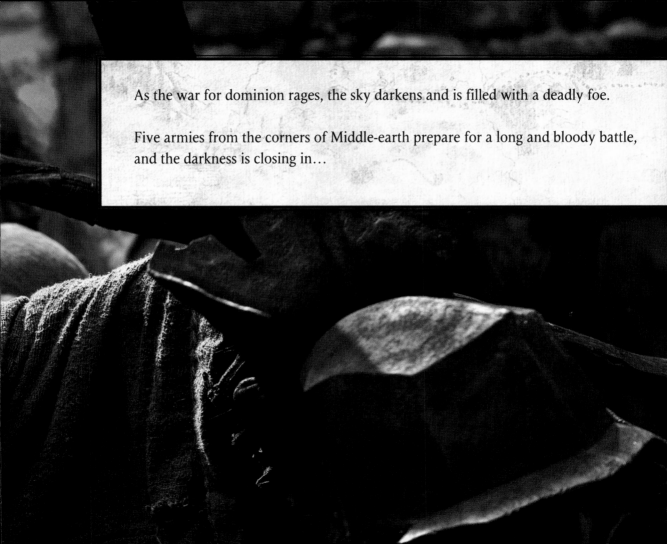

As the war for dominion rages, the sky darkens and is filled with a deadly foe.

Five armies from the corners of Middle-earth prepare for a long and bloody battle, and the darkness is closing in…

As the threat of devastation hangs over Middle-earth, King Thranduil can no longer hide in his Woodland Realm. Leading his skilled and deadly army, the Mirkwood Elves are a powerful threat to Azog's forces.

Thorin Oakenshield knows that he must take out the commander of the army; he must be the one to destroy Azog the Defiler.

As dark shapes fill the sky casting shadows upon the slopes of the mountain, Gandalf's hopes rest upon the help of some of the greatest protectors of Middle-earth.

Appointed leader of Lake-town, Bard the Bowman rallies his people to find whatever weapons they can in the ruins of Dale.

After losing their homes in Lake-town, his people must rebuild the once great city of Dale, so that the streets may once more be filled with much joy, laughter and prosperity.

But first, they must rid the streets of Dale of the monstrous Orcs and Goblins that seek to destroy them all….

As war rages between the five armies, the fate of Middle-earth hangs precariously in the balance… and Bilbo looks towards The Shire, wondering whether he will ever again see his beloved Bag End.

Who will be crowned King Under the Mountain, and will Sauron become the ruler of all?